This book belongs to

_____

_____

Christine Thompson-Wells
Author, Qualified Professional, Accredited Educator &
Independent Writer
BA Education, Dip of Teaching, MACEA

We support Diabetes Type One & Motor Neuron Disease. 10% of the net sales will be divided equally between both charities.

Our Mission:

Every child and adult have value and is important to us; therefore, we strive through online education and book publishing, to bring life-skill education to all children and all families.

For Education Packages

See our book websites: www.how2books.com.au and
www.fullpotentialtraining.com.au
or Contact:
admin@fullpotentialtraining.com.au

Changing lives through knowledge

HORMONES WITH HATS

MEETING CURRICULUM OBJECTIVES – UNITED KINGDOM (UK)

Natural body changes for boys between School Years 4 to 6, ages 9-11 years.

(Health and Wellbeing, Relationships, and Living in the Wider World)

Relationships Education, Relationships and Sex Education (RSE) and Health Education.

'Effective RSE does not encourage early sexual experimentation. It should teach young people to understand human sexuality and to respect themselves and others. It enables young people to mature, build their confidence and self-esteem and understand the reasons for delaying sexual activity. Effective RSE also supports people, throughout life, to develop safe, fulfilling, and healthy sexual relationships, at the appropriate time.'[1]

CURRICULUM OBJECTIVES – AUSTRALIA

Incorporating and supporting Years 4-6, ages 9-11 years. Personal, Social and Community Health (ACPPS070 – ACPS076 - ACPPS071 - ACPPS072 - ACPPS073 – and other related areas of the Curriculum including: TLF-IDM021182 Scootle.edu.au).

For School and family packages, please see Pages 77-78 for further information.

---

[1] Relationships and Sex Education (RSE) (Secondary) - GOV.UK (www.gov.uk)
Extracted from 'statutory guidance Relationships Education, Relationships and Sex Education (RSE) and Health Education & Australia: https://www.scootle.edu.au

If you have purchased this book without its cover, it may be a stolen book.

Neither the publisher or the author is under any obligation to provide professional services in anyway, legal, health or in any form which is related to this book, its contents advice or otherwise.

The law and practices vary from country to country and state to state.

If legal or professional information is required, the purchaser, or the reader should seek the information privately and best suited to their particular needs, and circumstances.

This is not a medical book. It is a book developed by the publisher to open the conversation about how the human body changes when growing up.

The author and publisher specifically disclaim any liability that may be incurred from the information within this book.
All rights reserved. No part of this book, including the interior design, images, cover design, diagrams, or any intellectual property (IP), icons and photographs may be reproduced or transmitted in any form by any means (electronic, photocopying, recording or otherwise) without the prior permission of the publisher. ©

Copyright© 2022 MSI Australia

All rights reserved.

ISBN: 978-0-6450890-3-5

Published by How2Books
Under licence from MSI Ltd, Australia
Company Registration No: 96963518255
NSW, Australia

See our website: www.how2books.com.au
Or contact by email: sales@how2books.com.au
Covers and Copyright owned by MSI, Australia

MSI acknowledges the author and images, text and photographs used in this book.

Children's books

Will Jones Space Adventures & The Money Formula – Book
Will Jones Space Adventures & The Money Formula – The Play
Will Jones & The Money Formula – Educator's Resource Pack
Will Jones Space Adventures & the Zadrilian Queen – Book
Will Jones Space Adventures & The Zadrilian Queen – Play
Will Jones Space Adventures & The Zadrilian Queen – Educator's Resource Pack
There are many more Will Jones Books To Come Out
Dora Damper Makes Honey Damper Bread
Potato Pete Goes to Market
Changes Facing Rosie
Changes Facing Kian
Changes Facing Jai
Changes Facing Caitlin

Books For Adults

Devils In Our Food
Recipes Without Devil Additives
How To Reduce Stress – Find Your Positive Head Space
Making Cash Flow
Selling Made Easy
Know Your Destination 'Go' Learn To Drive Your Mind
The Golden Book Of Whispering Poems and many more books.
Please see our website

Disclaimer

This is not a medical book and should not be used as such. The contents have been developed through observational theory and research (observational psychology). Information is also drawn from scientific literature, web search and personal enquiry.

The diagrams are for information and to enhance the meaning of the written text. Statements, information, and ideas within this book are for education purposes only. The text presented allows the reader to draw their own conclusions on the content offered.

Always consult with your doctor for possible illness or underlying illness. Christine Thompson-Wells (MSI) Australia, How2Books.com.au and Full Potential Training.com.au, cannot be held liable for any errors or omissions.

PREFACE

The characters and story within this book are fictitious. If a similar name or identity is drawn from within the writing, it is purely coincidental. The stories are not representative of any one or more individuals. The stories come together through my own unique and individual teaching and life experiences that are brought together to create this book.

Because all children worldwide go through similar bodily changes at similar times growing up, the stories connect with different children worldwide. The places where children are living are used to ground the story. The locations are destinations I have visited on my own life journey.

Each book targets different age and growth spans, and the story base incorporates children's stories, considering, some artistic thought, and writing.

The four books (two for boys and two for girls) are within the series: 'Changes', Children Growing Up, have been designed in a narrative form: (story telling) to assist children and to allow them to naturally adapt to their environment while they go through the different child to adult stages.

It is with sensitivity, that I acknowledge different cultures and traditions, this, and to my best ability, is understood in the writing, illustrations, and storytelling.

HOW TO USE THIS BOOK

In a NEW and exciting approach, hormone characters help our children learn about how their body changes when growing up.

The chapters are the story book. This approach allows the young person to come to grips with how their body and the way they think is changing.

Part two introduces the adults to the story and the information the young person has learnt.

Part three allows both the young adult and older adults to work through the pages together. This process helps the family to celebrate the changes that all young people go through as they go into adulthood.

We encourage both boys and girls to read the four books as they go through their own life changes.

Christine

Contents   Page

PREFACE
How To Use This Book

INTRODUCTION – The Story

Chapter One	1
Kian Has Changes	
Chapter Two	6
Boys' Talk	
Chapter Three	13
Getting Ready For Change	
Chapter Four	19
Getting To Know More	
Chapter Five	32
Chemicals Make The Difference	
Chapter Six	36
The Day Of The Big Game	
Part Two	
Working Together For Kids And Adults	45
Part Three	
Working Together For Kids And Adults	50
Let's Move On	51
Your Boy Child	53
Hormones. How? and Why?	59
A Boy's Progression Stages	62
How Kids Learn – Developing Life Skills	65
Establishing Healthy Habits	68

Your Boy and His Brain	71
Active Hormones, Personal Hygiene, Wellbeing, and Puberty	72
Role Models and Mentors	75
Understanding How The Human Body Grows and Matures & Relationships	76
Online School Packages	77
Family Packages	78

INTRODUCTION

This is the first book in the series of two books for boys. 'Changes' Facing Kian is a story about a young orphan boy, born in Iran. With no related family found and after the sudden death of his parents in a tragic car accident in the United Kingdom, he is put up for adoption.

Kian lives with his adopted family in Edinburgh, Scotland. The story is situated during the Covid Pandemic, 2020. The pandemic is not the focus of the story but is worked into the story as a 'reality check'.

Kian is starting to realise that he is changing, during these times and when he stops to think about himself, he often thinks about his biological parents. When not reflecting on the past, most of Kian's life, is spent with his, always busy, adopted family. Kian has a great relationship with his family, his mum teaches math and science at a local high school and his dad is an electrical engineer. He has two brothers and two sisters.

Kian loves football and has a good football coach called Mr Thomson. Before the training sessions, Mr Thomson talks to the boys about different growth times that happen when kids are growing up.

Chapter One
Kian Has Challenges

Kian lives in Edinburgh, Scotland; Scotland is based at the Northern part of the British Isles.

He lives with his adopted family of four children, a mum and dad, two dogs, two cats and a budgerigar.

He has two brothers and two sisters. One brother is a bit older and one a bit younger. His sisters are younger siblings, one is six, and one is five years old.

Kian has a good family with love and friendship. He is the only adopted child and does feel a bit different because of his adoption. He is nine years old. Because Kian was born of different parents, his skin is a little darker than his siblings and his hair is a little curly. Not very curly, just curly enough for Kian to comb it straight when it is wet!

Kian is a bit curious about his life and knows that one day he will search to learn more about his biological parents and the country he was born in.

His parents and family are great for Kian to be part of, they laugh a lot and have 'good fun' times together. 'Holidays are especially good...', Kian thinks. But he still has a nagging feeling about his birth or natural family.

Kian's schoolwork is going very well. He plays a lot of sport and supports his football team when he can. His dad, Kian, and two brothers often go to a local game, but his favourite team is *'Celtic but the tickets for those games are a bit expensive, with taking the four of us to a big game...!'* his dad says.

Every now and again, his dad would find the extra money to give the boys a treat.

Kian and his family live in a nice part of Edinburgh, not too rich and not too poor. Kian's mum teaches math and science at the local high school and his dad works as an electrical engineer. His dad also coaches in the Junior football team for the local area.

Kian's birth parents had migrated to the United Kingdom when he was a tiny baby. In a tragic car accident, both of his parents were killed. With no next of kin and any of his birth family to be found, Kian, was put up for adoption. This is how his adopted family found Kian.

Susie, his youngest sister of his adopted family, will be starting school in September. It is now late August and Susie is excited about her new school uniform. Susie, her mum and older sister have just got home from the shops where their mum has bought Susie's new uniform. She wants to show Kian her uniform and says, *'Kian, look at this, this is my new school uniform.'* While trying to show Kian her uniform, she was trying to put her backpack onto her back to give Kian the full picture of how she will look on her first day at school.

Kian looks at his little sister struggling with the backpack and quickly says, *'Sis,* (he calls her by her nickname) *come here and let me help you with your backpack!'*

He helps to get the pack onto her back, then gently turns her around to face him, he looks directly into her tiny face and says, *'Sis, you look so little and too little to wear such a big backpack!'*

This is not what Susie had wanted to hear. After all, she was now big enough to go to school and thought she was as big as her brothers and sisters!

Kian's mum overhears his comment and says, *'Kian, that's exactly what I said to you when I first saw you in your school uniform just about four years ago!'* With that last comment, Susie and her mum went downstairs.

Kian was also getting himself ready for school in the new term. In his bedroom, he was thinking about his new class and the new people he would meet, it didn't feel comfortable, but he knew that moving up to a new class with new students was what he had to do.

Kian had done so well with his last term school results; he had been moved up a grade and knew that he had a lot of work ahead of him. His older brother had been in Kian's new class last year and knew that his brother had worked hard to maintain his high school marks.

With so much going on in Kian's household, there was never time to feel sad or stay gloomy for long!

As Kian sat on his bed, he had just finished tidying his room as his dad had requested, he then heard the front door open and knew his brothers and dad had arrived home. There was so much noise coming from downstairs, that Kian also found himself running down the stairs and into the kitchen where the family was talking and laughing together.

His older brother, Ethan says, 'Guess what Kian, dad has tickets to go to the next Celtic match, next year.' Kian hearing this, replied, 'wow, that's great news, how did you get hold of those tickets', dad?'

Kian's dad replied, 'Well, I have a mate at an engineering company, he was offered some tickets, he cannot make that game, so he's offered them to us! As you know, the girls aren't interested in football and your mother would rather watch a netball match, so I have three extra tickets left, do you know a friend that you would like to take to this game, this same offer I have also mentioned to your brothers?'

Kian thought for a bit and then replied, '*Yes, I would like to take Arthur. He's a good friend and it would be a treat for him. He loves football but his dad loves cricket...!*'

The game was a long way off, and the world was also experiencing the Covid pandemic.

When the pandemic numbers were low, Kian's family wore masks when they went shopping and to school. When the numbers of sick people became higher, a 'lockdown' was enforced. Through this time, sports gatherings and football matches did not take place and for Kian's dad to now have tickets for a real game was a treat for the boys.

Over the Covid period, the children had online learning and Kian's mum would often sit at the kitchen table, instructing her students through online education.

Chapter Two
Boys' Talk

The research and development of the vaccine was in progress but unavailable at the time. The health and government announcements assured that a vaccine was being developed.

At Kian's household, the kitchen was a busy place at most times of the day, but with the excitement of the news of the tickets for the Celtic match, the atmosphere in the kitchen was buzzing and electric!

Susie's news of her new school uniform didn't seem like news to anybody else but Susie! Kian, sensing his little sister's feelings, stopped everybody when he said, *'We have some other great news also, Sis has her new school uniform and her backpack...!'* With this announcement, she ran upstairs, into her bedroom and came downstairs carrying everything from her new school coat, uniform, socks, shoes, and backpack. She wanted to show the family everything that had been bought that day.

The family stopped in their tracks while their little sister and the baby of the house, went through, with fine description, every item she would need for school.

When Susie had finished showing everybody her new clothes, Kian's mum, keeping her excitement under control, then announced, 'mmm...everybody, please out of my kitchen, I have work to do and I'm sure that everybody else has jobs to do. We also need wood chopped for the boiler; it's going to be a cold winter. Kian, Ethan, 'their mum said, '...you can help your dad in the garden with the wood and then help him to tidy up the yard!'

The northern autumn was starting early. The leaves of the trees had started to change their colour and during the evening there was a chill in the air. The days could still be sunny and warm, but they could also be very wet when the long, wet days set in.

With the boys and Kian's dad out of the kitchen, Mary, Kian's mum, had room to move.

She then looked at the girls and said, '...what are you two going to do this afternoon? Anna, the older of the two girls said, 'I want to start to read the new book we bought today.' Their mum replied, 'that's a good idea! And Susie, what are you going to do?' Susie looked at her mum with her big blue eyes and bouncing blond curls said, 'mummy, I'm going to play with my dolls house!'

Their mum replied, '...that's good to hear. I will start to make a casserole for dinner tonight, but you girls might like to join me when I start making the apple pies. I hope you haven't forgotten; we will quickly take some pies to Gramps and Nanna after they are baked. As you know because of the pandemic, *we cannot go into their house, but we will talk to them from the street when we leave the pies!'*

Susie had forgotten about Gramps and Nanna and when she heard she would see them tonight, she felt very happy.

Both girls left their mother in the kitchen, where they could hear her from downstairs, chopping vegetables and occasionally the knocking and sounds of pots either going into the sink or being put on the table or stove.

Then the smell of their mum's cooking drifted up the stairs. Their mum, when she had time, also liked to make homemade bread and scones. The family loved their mum's cooking and everything, home cooked, was eaten – no crumbs, were ever left-over, nothing ever remained!

Kian's mum had often said, after a meal was served and eaten, *'...it's like a vacuum cleaner coming through the house, the food just disappears!'* The family had heard this so much, they took no notice of it when their mum made the comment.

Little Susie played with her dolls house for a short time and then got onto her bed and fell asleep. Stretching out on her bed, her sister Anna continued reading her book.

The three boys and their dad worked in the garden. Their dad cut up the wood collected from the forest a week ago, while Kian and Ethan and their younger brother Tim, raked up leaves and tidied the garden while removing or cutting dead branches from the trees.

Kian wanted to talk to Ethan, and through their work in the garden, he found the perfect opportunity.

Kian, said, 'Ethan, can I talk to you?' Ethan, looked at his brother and said, 'sure, what's on your mind?'

The boys started to talk about different things and especially Kian's concern over the higher class he was going into next term at school. At this point, Kian's dad looked up from chopping the wood and could see the boys were in deep conversation. Unaware of their father watching them, the boys continued to talk.

Their father, eventually, joined them, and they all sat on the piles of chopped wood listening to what each other had to say.

The time passed and then, Mary, Kian's mum called out, 'would you like some biscuits and tea, I'm just about to make myself a cuppa?'

On a tray, Mary brought out the tea-filled cups and biscuits where they all sat talking.

It was a mild day and autumn was just starting to show itself. Mary looked at the tall trees in the back garden and said to her husband, *'Tom, winter is not so far away!'* Tom looked at the trees and nodded his head in agreement.

At that point, Mary shouts *'…. oops, I had better check that casserole otherwise it might burn!'*

Mary quickly collects up the empty cups and biscuit plate, puts them all on the tray and then walks into the kitchen to check the cooking casserole. *'All is good'*, she says out loud, *'…it hasn't burnt yet!'*

It was nearly time to start cooking the apple pies. From the kitchen, she walks upstairs and sees little Susie, on her bed, still sound asleep. Her sister is still busy reading her book!

She, Mary, not wanting to disturb Susie, quietly goes into Anna's room and says, *'do you still want to help me make the apple pies?'* and Anna replies, *'yes,' that would be great mum, I'll come downstairs with you.'*

Without a sound, Anna and her mum softly walk past Susie's room, where her mum looks in to see the sleeping child. All was well. The two make their way quietly down the stairs and close the kitchen door behind them.

Now was the time that Anna loved, working with her mum in the kitchen, chatting to her mum about all sorts of things as they made apple pies together.

Mary cut up the apples, leaving the skin on. She says to Anna, *'the skin is where the goodness is, so unless the apple is bad, keep the skin on the fruit.'* She continues, *'...the apples have been good this year, plenty of good fruit at affordable prices!'*

The apples and cinnamon are cooking on the stove and smell delicious. The smell is so good, the aroma reaches little Susie's bedroom, she wakes up and goes downstairs. She looks at her mother and sister and says, *'I want to help you make the pies!'*

Her mother picks up the child and gives her a hug and kiss on the cheek. As she does this she says, *'you were asleep my little sleepyhead, but you can help us now...!'*

The mother gently sits Susie on the kitchen chair in front of the large wooden table. Her mum then gives the child a glass of milk and a biscuit.

While the apples cooked, it was time to make the pastry and Anna loved making pastry. She liked the different shapes she could cut out and was amazed by the different types of flour her mum used.

After their garden jobs were finished, the boys and their dad came in from their garden work. Tom announced, *'this kitchen smells good, when is dinner ready?'*

Mary and Anna were now ready to put the cooked apple into the uncooked, pastry, pie bottoms. The bottoms were ready for the cooked apple to be spooned into the case. Then the pie top would be put into place.

While this was happening, Tom and the boys went into watch the re-run of the football game from last Saturday's football game in the back garden! Tom always made his point as he watched the boys' movements and the way they kicked the ball!

Chapter Three
Getting Ready For Changes

With some of the Covid restrictions lifted, it was time to resume school!

Kian was getting ready for his first day back to school and going to his new and higher class; he was nervous and knew that his brother was in this same class this time last year!

He was now at school, and the first day back after the half-term holidays and the last term of the year. Kian had been told by his previous teacher, *'...you will be going to a new class after the half-term holiday.'* Kian had done so well in his last tests was the reason for the move. Nervous about the move, he now needed to be brave enough to work with the situation.

Ethan met Kian during the breaktime and asked, *'How is it going?'* Kian replied, *'OK, I think, but I have known some of the kids from before, we have often kicked a ball together, so it's not that bad. But I think I am going to have to work hard; these kids seem smart!'*

Ethan, looking squarely into Kian's face, replied, *'Don't worry Bro, you can do it; you're as smart as any of them and don't let any of them intimidate you!'*

With his brother's words of encouragement, Kian went back to his class once the bell had rung.

Kian had done exceedingly well in his last term's math, biology, and science tests and therefore he had been moved up a class.

His brother Ethan was in his last year at the school and would be going to high school next year, Kian still had another eighteen months to go before he would be going to a high school.

The lesson for science began and instantly, Kian felt he was alone in the classroom, he was completely at home with the information; he could clearly see the concept and facts, and instantly understood what his teacher was saying. 'Mr. McPherson', Ethan had said, *'is an excellent science teacher, he's so good, he should be teaching at high school!'*

Kian paid attention for the whole lesson, never once taking his mind off the information being spoken about by the teacher.

That night, Kian got home a bit later because he wanted to speak to Mr. McPherson after school. The family were all home by the time Kian got home.

He had taken the bus to school. On the way home, he waited such a long time for the bus to come, he had decided he would ride his bike tomorrow!

His mum was also back teaching and met Kian at the front door, 'Hi Kian...' she says, 'how was the day?' As they both walk through the open front door together, Kian starts to tell his mum about his busy day. Now in the kitchen, she waits while she listens to Kian's story. After Kian had finished telling his mum about his day, she lifts her heavy school bag onto the kitchen table and then Kian dumps his on the kitchen floor.

Kian's mum pours Kian a glass of milk, and as she does so, both Anna and Susie come running through the back kitchen door. The girls had been home for a while. On busy days, their dad meets them from school. Before the covid pandemic, the girls would be met by the neighbour, who also had children at the same school, and they would all walk home together. They would stay with the neighbour until either their mum or dad arrived home.

As Kian's mum turned around, she now saw Susie and Anna, come through the open kitchen door with their dad closely following. Their mum threw her arms out so that both girls could run to their mum and have a hug and a kiss.

The kitchen was slowly filling up with people.

Drinking his milk, Kian, stops, puts his glass down on the table, and then pours a glass of milk each for the girls. As the girls and Kian drank their milk, Kian's brothers arrive home. After a pause, Kian's dad, quickly says, '...that's good, we are all home together, there is a wild storm and wild weather on its way!'

It was a storm like no other, the electricity was cut from falling trees being uprooted and falling onto power lines; a tree in the back garden fell sideways onto a neighbour's shed, and hail hit the glass windowpanes cracking some around the house.

Without any electricity in the house, Tom, Kian's dad said, *'let's collect some dry wood, light the fire and cook some toast, that will do for dinner tonight!'*

The boys knew exactly where the dry wood was stored; the three boys ran out into the garden and into the heavily falling rain.

The lightening cracked in the sky above them, then the banging and crashing of the thunder shook the ground as they stood loading the dry wood up into their arms. Once loaded up, the boys quickly ran back into the house.

Their mum had found some frozen crumpets in the freezer and had bought, freshly baked bread on the way home from school.

Cutting chunky pieces of bread from the loaf in the candlelight was something different for the children to experience. Anna wanted the end of the bread toasted; she called it *'The Nobby'* while Susie wanted the softer bread inside the loaf toasted!

The boys just wanted big pieces of toast with lashings of butter and anything they wished on the top. Tom, Kian's dad said, 'my we are having a feast, you forget how freshly cut bread, toasted can be so delicious!'

As the candlelight flickered, the food on the table could be seen! There were, different packets of cheese, some honey in jars, some left-over meat from the lunches that were made the night before, and in the middle of the table sat the last of the remaining apple pies, and in the jug, the remaining custard.

Mary was relieved for the storm, it meant she didn't have to cook dinner, this meant she could get on with marking her students' papers and thought, 'I'll have all of my work done early tonight, that makes a nice change, I might just have an early night!'

With dinner over and the lights still out, the family headed to their bedrooms for an early night. As Tom and Mary headed to bed, they shouted their usual, 'Good night' and the chorus from the children replied.

As Tom got into bed, he said to Mary, 'I think we will all be in for a big clean up tomorrow, we may have to keep the boys at home to help. Old Mr and Mrs. MacLeod, next door may need a hand to tidy up!'

After the big storm, there was a lot of cleaning up to do, with that done, school resumes.

With everyone now back at work and school, Kian goes to his second class of biology, and then on to science; both are some of his favourite subjects and looks forward to this time.

Chapter Four
Getting To Know More

Kian didn't understand why he felt so excited about the second classes of science and math for this term, but he did.

It was still only September and the shops he passed on the way to school were filling their windows with Christmas stock; he couldn't help but take the time to stop and look at some of the amazing things appearing in the windows for this Christmas!

The first class was science. Mr McPherson was busy marking papers when the class arrived. They waited at the door, where some of the children lined up in the que, were misbehaving. Mr McPherson did not take any nonsense and those caught misbehaving usually had time to spend with him after school!

Mr McPherson could hear the noise coming from a group of students at the back of the que. He got up from his seat and quietly went to the noisy group and gave out notes to each student involved – he then said, *'I have your names, see me in my class after school!'*

The line of students fell silent while they waited for Mr McPherson to allow them into the room. Once the group was silent, Mr McPherson, waved his hand and the students quietly entered the room and went to their desks.

Mr McPherson stood in front of his students with his arms crossed and patiently waited for everyone to be ready.

Mr McPherson was an older teacher who wore tweed suits, smart shirts, and ties, 'he was the old school….!' Kian's mum had once said.

The lesson was over, and Kian was heading to his math class. As he entered the class, 'he couldn't help thinking how smart some of the kids were…!' He then thought about what Ethan had previously said to him…!

With the school day finished and all his subjects for the day over, it was now time to go to football training. The coach for the team's training is also a teacher, he also teaches biology at another school in Edinburgh.

Before each session, the boys are given a short lesson on either hygiene, biology, or useful information that the boys can think about.

The coach, Mr. Thomson, said loudly as the boys were getting changed, 'Boys, QUIET please, before we get onto the pitch tonight, I want to quickly talk to you about testosterone', with this the boys giggled and made comments. Mr Thomson, shouted again, 'Come on boys, some common sense please…!'

He continued, *'last week we spoke about your personal growth ...and we saw this little character on the screen'*. He shows the image of the growth hormone the boys were now familiar with.

He continues, *'...you also learnt that this hormone is not only known as a growth hormone but is also known as somatotropin. That's a big word so just remember, "growth hormone"'*.

Mr Thomson now wants to talk about testosterone. He waits for the boys to settle down and to become quiet. He waits, and waits, then says, *'Boys the longer I wait for you to settle down the less time you will have to play football...!'* The boys instantly pay attention and wait to see the next image shown on the screen.

He again waits for a response. The quietness of the room can be heard, 'you could hear a pin drop...' Mr Thomson thinks to himself!

The image of testosterone is now on the screen. The boys are quiet, very quiet! Then one of the boy's says, *'Mr Thomson, we didn't know that testosterone was a Celtic player...!'*

Mr Thomson laughs a little and moves from foot to foot.

He then continues, *'both boys and girls have and make testosterone in their bodies, but boys have, normally, and make more than girls. Mr Thomson continues, 'another hormone I would like to mention is, Gonadotropin, but we will talk about that at the next meeting.'* With this, the boys start to giggle again. One noisy boy shouts out, *'hey Smithy,* did you know that?' Mr Thomson then says loudly, '...remember boys, you will have less playing time if you continually interrupt me...!'

The boys settle down again. Mr Thomson says, 'testosterone, is produced in the cells of an embryo after about eight weeks. The embryo, as you know, is the start of making a baby.'

Again, the loud boy makes a comment, 'hey, Wilson, did you know that you started becoming a boy when you were eight weeks old, how about that?'

The boys were laughing and having fun. Mr Thomson knew it was time for the boys to play the game, 'they were too boisterous to settle down' thought Mr Thomson.

Mr Thomson continues after some order was restored again, 'The last thing I want to quickly say to you this afternoon is about testosterone, testosterone will add to your strength. Some of you boys are bigger than the boys you are playing football with, though you are all the same age, so please remember, football is not only a game; it also includes showing respect for your fellow teammates.'

Before Mr Thomson allows the boys to leave the dressing room, he wants to make one last comment. 'Finally,' he says, 'Some of you will notice that you may be starting to grow some body hair on your body; this is because testosterone is now being released into your body!'

Mr Thomson waited for the loud boy to make a comment, but he did not. With the silence now in the room and with Mr Thomson's last comments, the boys ran out onto the field and practised their ball kicking techniques while they warmed up before the game.

After the game, the boys showered before going home.

Kian had ridden his bike to school and then to the football training. He had a bit of a ride home, he rode down two country lanes covered in gold and brown fallen autumn leaves, past his school and onto the home straight. He arrived just in time for dinner.

Kian's dad was eager to know about his training and quickly asked, *'how did you go with your training son, did you win, and did you have a good game?'*

Kian sniffed the air, he was starving and thought to himself, 'that food smells great!'. He then answered his dad, *'yes, dad it was a good match, no, we didn't win. The boys mucked up a bit and were laughing about testosterone.'*

Kian's mum overhearing his reply looked at her husband, then asked Kian, as she served up homemade burgers and chips with fried tomatoes and mushrooms, *'...why should they muck up because of the word testosterone?'*

Kian feeling sheepish replied, *'I don't know mum, it's just boys…!'*

Kian's family had often had discussions about words and how important they were to understand and the correct meaning and usage of the word, so for Kian to hear the word testosterone, during any lessons or conversations, it wasn't a strange word or big thing within their family conversations!

After dinner when the family were sitting at the kitchen table, Kian's sisters had a shower and got ready for bed. Kian's dad, each night, told the girls a story before they went to sleep.

During the evening time of the family being together, it was the time, that each person spoke about their day.

The three boys and their mum clean the kitchen table after the meal, and put the salt, pepper, and sauces back into their right place in the kitchen cupboard.

As the boys cleaned away the dirty plates, each person spoke about their day and experiences. This was the time to bring Kian's experience at school and during football training into the discussion.

Kian had crumpled the handouts from Mr McPherson into his school bag before the game and now bent down to retrieve the paperwork to show the family.

While this was going on, Kian's mum, Mary, went upstairs to say *'good night'* to the girls.

By the time their parents were back downstairs, and in the kitchen, the table was cleared and wiped, the dishwasher was humming in the background and the family sat around the table ready to talk about their day.

Also, by this time, Kian had his paper handouts ready to show the family.

Kian displayed the paperwork on the kitchen table from the Coach and explained, *'...we have learnt about the growth hormone before, Mr. McPherson said, testosterone, is a male hormone but girls also have testosterone'. He continued, 'the embryo starts out as a girl, and it isn't until after about eight weeks that the Y chromosome in the cells start to work. Kian's, mum looks at the boys and says, 'Yes, that's right Kian. It is at that point the girl embryo starts to become a boy. This happens because testosterone, like other hormones, is the male hormone. We have many different hormones in our bodies, they allow our body to grow and develop.'*

YOUR NOTES
Name at least 3 times in your life when you have gone through a growth spurt.

1) ....
2) ....
3) ....

Both boys and girls make testosterone in their bodies It is an important hormone because it helps both boys' and girls' bodies to stay healthy and to become stronger.

Kian's dad picks up the handouts and says, *'It's difficult to think that we have so much chemistry running around inside our bodies, and each of us may have similar chemicals, and how we all look and behave differently....!'*

Eager to show Kian's dad his other handouts, he reaches inside his bag and says, *'...dad, you might like to see these also, they were given out before the end of last term!'*

He continues talking to his family, *'it is also interesting that boys and girls both have estrogen and progesterone. I know girls have estrogen and progesterone, but I didn't realise that boys did...!'*

Each person around the table takes a turn to look at the illustrations on the table and then pass on the paperwork to a person sitting next to them.

Kian's mum then says, *'progesterone and estrogen are important hormones for both boys and girls, but they do work in different ways and in different amounts in both boys and girls!'*

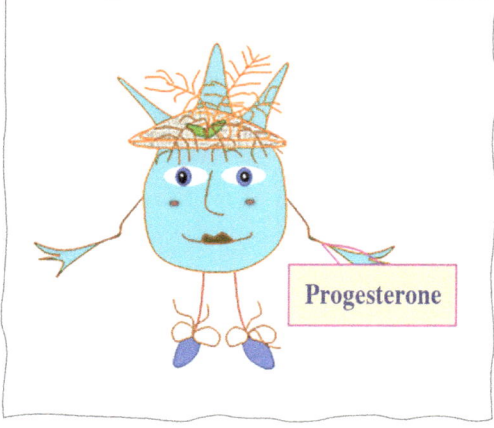

The last illustration to come out of Kian's bag was his picture of ghrelin. He said to his mum as he pulled the crumpled paper from the bottom of the bag, *'This is ghrelin, and is the hormone released from the stomach when we feel hungry, mum!'*

Kian's mum takes a minute to look at the picture on the table. She cautiously replies, *'...this hormone was only discovered in 1999, and is related to the growth hormone...!*

If we eat food when we are not hungry as in eating "junk food," eating can become a habit and that is when some people put on weight...!'

The family take a moment to look at the characters on the paper before them and then Tim, Kian's younger brother says, 'I wonder what hormones really look like? I don't know if I would want these hormones with their silly hats and signs inside my body...!'

The family again looked at the illustrations before them and each laughed when they thought about Tim's comment. It was now time for bed.

Quickly Kian replies, '...*there is another hormone that Mr. McPherson wants to introduce us to at the next football practise*' – he stopped talking, and looked at the family one by one, he then continued, '*it's gonadotropin, I think that is its name...!* He stops and thinks again and again and again. With such a pause, the family go in different directions to get ready for bed!

---

[2] Gonadotropins regulate the growth, development, and function of the reproductive organs.

Chapter Five
Chemicals Make The Difference

It was almost Christmas time and the Covid pandemic had worsened in the United Kingdom. A lot of schooling was done from home and Mary found she was spending more time with the children and home schooling them all.

Kian was encouraged by his football coach to practise in the back garden and the three boys often took time out by playing a bit of football. Within their practise, which they all took seriously, they became focused on the game they were playing. Sometimes the girls would join them and would try to compete with the boys, the boys often let them win a goal, they would eventually give up and go back inside the house and continue with what they were doing before joining the boys.

Tom, Kian's dad continued to work from his office and would often walk the long distance from their home to work rather than catching any public transport; this he was hoping, would reduce the possibilities of catching the virus!

Mary, Kian's mum, would frequently ring the elderly couple, Mr and Mrs MacLeod, next door, to make sure they were well and to see if they needed any groceries. When Mary would ring Gramps and Nanna, they would often ask, *'when are the next apple pies coming around?'*

During the pandemic, Mary and the children would call to see their grandparents once or twice a week. Each time, Mary would take them some freshly baked cakes, scones, pies, and other foods; they both looked forward to these treats from their daughter. They also looked forward to seeing their grandchildren. Though they all spoke from behind the front garden fence, keeping the gate well and truly locked, in front of them.

Christmas came and went. Most New Year celebrations were cancelled, this was to try and contain the virus, but the pandemic only got worse!

Kian, his brothers, and dad were hoping that the game in August would not be cancelled due to the pandemic.

During one of Kian's online biology sessions, he learnt about many chemicals and their role within the human body. He was becoming more and more interested in the subject. He also learnt that there are fifty-four identified hormones that work to keep the human body healthy.

The more Kian reads about hormones the greater his interest becomes.

New vaccines had been developed and 'it seems', thought Kian, 'that the world was holding its breath waiting for a way to stop the pandemic from spreading'. '...*not only that*,' he says out loud, '...*we want to go to the game with dad...!*'

After some time, school resumed and, though limited and with social distancing in place, some of Kian's practise football training also resumed.

The first day back at school was great for Kian and the boys. They left the house together and all rode their bikes.

The girls walked with their mum; they all walked to the school gate, their mum watched them go into school and then made her way to her high school where she had a busy day ahead of her.

As a teacher, Mary knew she would have some challenges. Because of the pandemic disruptions within education, Mary, knew the children would take some time to re-establish and return to regular behaviour.

Kian, too, was feeling a bit uncomfortable. Though he understood he was going into puberty, he was unsure of just how he would react to the changes his body was making. After school, that night and as he lay on his bed, looking out into the night sky, he spoke to himself, *'So, chemicals make us change, hormones aren't the only chemicals, there are different cells, molecules and hormones inside our bodies all working together!*

I know I'm changing but I don't know how I will be, sometimes I feel embarrassed, but my brother is older than me and he seems to manage it...!'

From my lessons, I know that chemicals are making these changes; but I feel nervous about this happening to me!'

Kian had decided to talk to Ethan and his dad.

Chapter Six
The Day Of The Big Game

The tension and excitement of the day was there, in the kitchen as the boys ate their breakfast, and while Kian, waited for his friend Arthur to join them; they would all go to the game together.

Ethan, said to Kian, 'What time is Arthur coming around?' Kian, replied, '*A little after lunch, his dad is dropping him off...*' The boys had homework and their household jobs to do before they went to the game, but the excitement was too much as they all ended up laughing at the silliest of comments.

Lunch came and went, and they were then, all on the way to the game. Joining the crowds wearing their green and white hats and scarves, the excitement was at fever pitch.

Mary had made some sausage sandwiches for them to eat at half-time; she also added some chocolate brownies, she hadn't mentioned to them.

It was a great game and as a treat, they went to the gelato shop in Edinburgh. Kian's dad, was so happy with the outcome of the game, he says, 'OK, *gelato on me...!*' The five made their way to a cubical in the gelato shop and sat down waiting for the ice cream to be served. Each gelato was served in a glass dish, some had strawberry with a lashing of strawberry sauce, others had chocolate and Kian's dad had, rich chocolate and cashew nuts, drizzled with homemade chocolate sauce!

They had all had such a great Saturday afternoon, they sat, talked, and laughed as they re-lived the game.

Kian's dad, then said to Arthur, '...*and Arthur, what school do you go to?*' Arthur told the group about his school and where he lived. He lived a bit out of Edinburgh and had met Kian at a friendly football match. Both boys instantly liked each other and so kept in touch.

Arthur continued, *'I love biology, and our teacher, Mrs Gray has told us so much about how we grow and change as we get older!'* Kian's dad replied, *'Kian, you were telling us about your biology class also, do you want to share it with Arthur?'*

Kian, listened to his dad, and replied, *'OK, sure dad, I can do that....!'*

Kian explained about the little characters Mr Thomson, his football coach, had drawn and how the boys had each been given handouts with explanations about what each character's (hormones), and the role they play within the human male body.

Kian stops talking and then says, as he stands up from the table to get a piece of paper out of his pocket, he undoes the paper, and shows Arthur, the testosterone image.

They all look at the character as Kian uncreased it and laid it out flat on the table.

Arthur, looked at the image before him, and replied, 'Kian, have you got another copy of this, because I would love to give it to Mrs Gray?'

Kian, quickly replied, 'No, take it, I have another, and if I don't, I'm sure Mr Thomson, would give me another copy...!'

Then, Kian's dad said, 'you've learnt a lot about other hormones also from Mr Thomson, if Arthur is interested, why don't you invite him around next Saturday and let his see your other copies?'

With this, it was time to finish at the gelato shop and time to get the bus home.

After a busy week at school, the family was having their usual Saturday morning breakfast of porridge, then toasted crumpets with honey. Kian's dad asked, '...is Arthur coming over today?' Kian, replied, 'I think about eleven dad...!' His dad replied, 'that's good to hear!'

Ethen was having his friend over too, while Tim, their mum and dad and the girls went to the park and then, to do some grocery shopping in town!

At about eleven that morning, there was a knock at the front door, Kian answered it, and both Arthur and James, Ethan's friend, were waiting together to be let into the house. Kian, welcomed the boys, and quickly said, 'Come in, it's great to see you both...!'

Kian showed Arthur to his room, where Kian had his schoolwork all over the place, but on his bed, he had the hormone images Mr Thomson had given as handouts!

As Arthur saw the characters strewn all over the bed, Arthur started to laugh...!

Kian looked at his friend, and he too, saw how funny the paper images looked.

Kian picks up the paper with the growth hormone image, and says, '...they are funny, let's look at some more....!'

'This is estrogen, both boys and girls have this hormone, but girls have more...! He continues, '...estrone, is a girls' hormone.'

Estradiol is also a boys' and girls' hormone...!' As he picks up other images, he says, 'here's another, this is estriol and a girls' hormone...!

'This, hormone, progesterone, both boys and girls have. Has your teacher told you about this one?' Arthur shakes his head, in a 'No' answer to Kian. Kian continues, '...well, apparently, it helps boys make testosterone...!' Kian sheepishly replies. Arthur, looks at Kian, and says, '...really, I didn't know that...!'

Kian says to Arthur, 'do you remember, this is testosterone, we all talked about that at the gelato shop last week?'

Arthur replies, 'I did show Mrs Gray your handout and she said, "they are very interesting, and she had not seen hormones ever explained like this before!"

Kian, then picks up the Ghrelin image, and says, '...Mr Thomson said about this hormone, and I didn't know that hormones send messages to your brain when you are hungry, but some food has so many additives and is so processed, ghrelin is released to your brain, even when you're not hungry, and that isn't good!'

Kian, continues, 'Mr Thomson, said last week, even animals have hormones, that's how they know when to mate with their partners; hormones tell them to find a mate and have babies, if they don't do that, animals, like birds, will die out, and become extinct. He said, through global warming, and pollution, many birds aren't responding because their natural habitats have been destroyed and therefore, the hormones aren't working in the animals...!'

With that mentioned, the boys went downstairs and into the garden where Ethen and James were kicking the football and all the boys joined in to have a game before lunch!

YOUR EXTRA NOTES

Part Two
WORKING TOGETHER
For kids and adults

KIDS' AND ADULTS' WORKSHEET

Why do you need to have growth hormones working in your body?

....
....
....
....
....

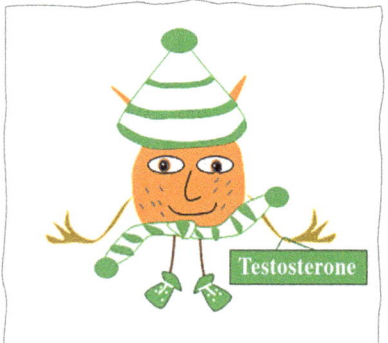

Boys normally have more testosterone in their body, why?

....
....
....
....
....

Girls have estrogen, but do boys?

....
....
....
....
....
....

Estradiol belongs to what hormone _ _ _ _ _ _ _ ?

....
....
....
....
....
....

Is estriol a girls' hormone?

....
....
....
....
....
....
....

Estrone belongs to what hormone _ _ _ _ _ _ _ ?

....
....
....
....
....
....

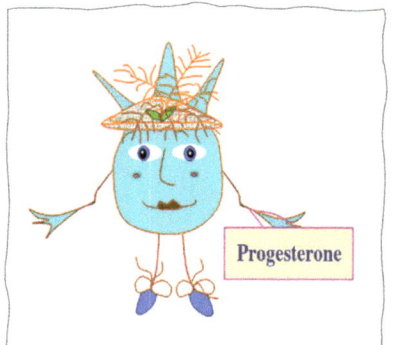

What is the benefit of having the hormone progesterone in your body?

....
....
....
....
....

All of the body's hormones play a role in keeping us healthy, what role does ghrelin play?

....
....
....
....

When you have more ghrelin in your body than your body needs, what does it make you do?

....
....
....
....
....

YOUR EXTRA NOTES

....
....
....
....
....
....
....
....
....
....
....
....
....
....
....
....
....
....
....

Part Three
WORKING TOGETHER
For kids and adults

LET'S MOVE ON

In the 21st Century, we need to take a realistic approach to our natural brain and body growth and the evolution we have gone through in the last four to seven million years. The myths and old attitudes, that limit healthy growth and wellbeing should now be left where they belong – in the past.

We now have technology that supports the science we can all work from. If for instance, it was previously thought that the human brain was fully developed and mature at birth, this is now proven to be completely wrong. The human brain does not mature until a young person is in their mid-twenties.

From before birth, this unique tool needs to be protected until the young person can understand what they have inside their head. They need to understand its growth from the beginning to their age of maturity and into later life.

There is a lot to be said for the American guidelines: young people can legally drink when they are 21 years of age and not before. Alcohol can and is proven to damage the growing brain. This fact alone should put all adults, parents, grandparents, older young adults, and carers on alert.

When an adult gives a young person, 'just a sip of wine!' or any alcohol of any kind, they are doing a great injustice to that person, and their future, and may cause irreversible brain damage; is a 'sip of alcohol' worth this?

As adults, whether you are a parent, grandparent or indeed do not have children of your own, we are all responsible, as a community, for the wellbeing of our young people. No one adult can avoid this responsibility.

It is time to take our heads out of the sand and to improve, right now, the future for our young people and the future generations.

We have seen, over the years, and more recently, shown by some young and older people, the lack of respect for other people, including females, people with differences and different customs within our communities; this is not only in Australia but continues to happen worldwide. This lack of respect has been and is being bred into national cultures.

Young people also need to understand respect and responsibility for their own body and brain, once this is done, it will reduce drug taking and the taking of other mind-altering substances.

Worldwide, the quality of the future will depend on the children being educated today.

YOUR BOY CHILD

- Boys from the embryonic stage, through development in the womb and then to birth, are different to girls.

- A male baby's body produces testosterone from an early age; this makes a difference to how the brain develops. From lying within the bassinet, crib, or cot, a boy can show interest in mechanical toys such as trucks, lorries, trains, cranes, or cars.

- By comparison to girls, boys' brains grow slower and develop differently; boys usually catch up to girls by the age of eighteen years.

- All human conceptions and for the first eight weeks, resemble the developing girl child. Through cell growth and the development of the Y chromosome within the cells, testosterone starts to be produced. This production encourages the penis and testicles to grow and develop. By the fifteenth week, they are fully developed.

- To keep the penis clean and healthy, the growing boy child will have erections while in the womb; this is a natural cleaning and healthy function for the organ.

- During pregnancy, and when the testes are formed, testosterone will continue to be made by the testes.

At the time of the birth, the testosterone testosterone level within the baby's blood will be that of a twelve- to thirteen-year-old, puberty male. Male babies need high levels of testosterone to allow their bodies to develop the male qualities needed to make boy babies.

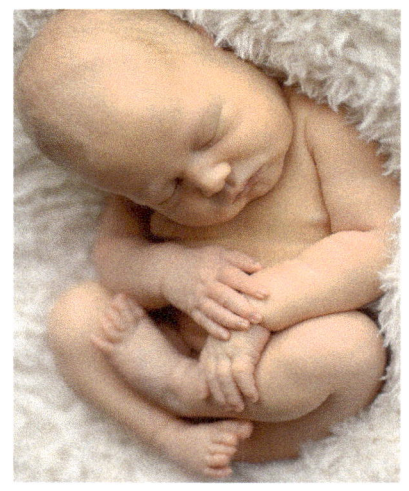

Image courtesy of Pixabay

➤ After birth and by the age of three months, a baby's testosterone level will start to decline and will re-emerge by the age of four. At this age, it is his time of interest for cars, trucks, loud noises, running and jumping and being a typical boy. This testosterone rush will start to decline as he reaches five and settles down in time for school.

(From my own experience with a baby boy, regardless of age, our son was always attracted to any form of engine, motor or building toys).

> Testosterone starts to re-emerge between the ages seven to eight and in time for puberty. In a healthy child and into older male adulthood, testosterone will continue to be produced until death.

When a baby boy is born, and like girls, the genital area of boys is in miniature.

This is no surprise as all babies need time to grow and develop after birth. In boys, the penis is short and in proportion to their body size.

In an uncircumcised boy, the penis foreskin is left in place after birth. In a circumcised boy, the outer end of the foreskin is removed.

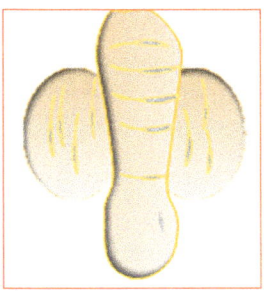

In this diagram, and at the birth of a baby boy, it can be seen how the foreskin of the penis is left in place. The scrotum, the skin's sack keeping the testes in place, may also appear larger and loose, keeping the testes safe. As the child grows and develops, the scrotum will tighten up until the time of puberty.

The hormone, testosterone is produced in the testes of the male and the ovaries of females. It is also produced in the adrenal glands of both females and males.

Testosterone is the main hormone in the male sperm supply. Sperm will start to be produced by the testes as the child enters puberty; and as said, *'it can be as early as seven to eight years'*, but normally about eight!

As the boy grows, so too, does his genital area, this allows his body to function properly. During puberty and at different times, through the day and night, a boy will experience different arousal levels from the penis. This is both healthy and natural.

Between these ages, the male might experience different and mild growth spurts, maybe some hair will appear on the body or in and round the genital area, and under the arms.

The scrotum will start to expand to allow the testes to do their work in making sperm, but the expansion also allows the testes to keep cool during hot weather, or if the body experiences excessive heat.

In this diagram, the scrotum is seen, dotted lines, and shows the expansion of the skin. As previously explained, this is a natural occurrence to keep the testes cool.

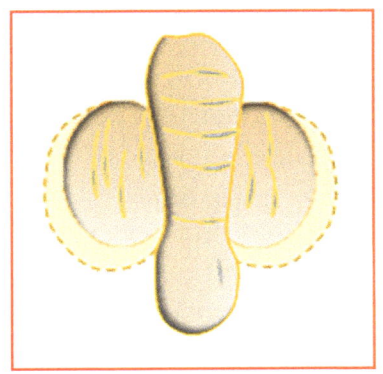

In a cool climate, if the testes experience cooling or coldness, the scrotum will tighten up.

Both loose and a tighter scrotum are made by nature for protection of the testes.

To allow the transference of sperm, the testes need to be connected to the penis through the Vas deferens, a pair of tube-like structures linking the testes to the urethra.

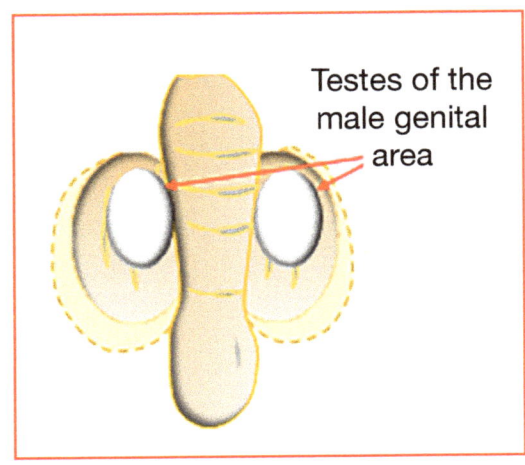

Testes of the male genital area

The vas deferens transports mature sperm to the urethra in preparation for ejaculation.

Not all sperm go on the journey and leave the penis, some sperm die and are absorbed back into the body; this again, is a natural process that allows the body to make good use what it has made. In the below diagram, you can see a simplified outline of how the penis, testes, and body functions when puberty is about to happen.

For a child to be faced with all the processes of how its body works seems a bit premature, but this is the will of nature, nature takes over, this in turn, protects your child and makes them ready for entering puberty.

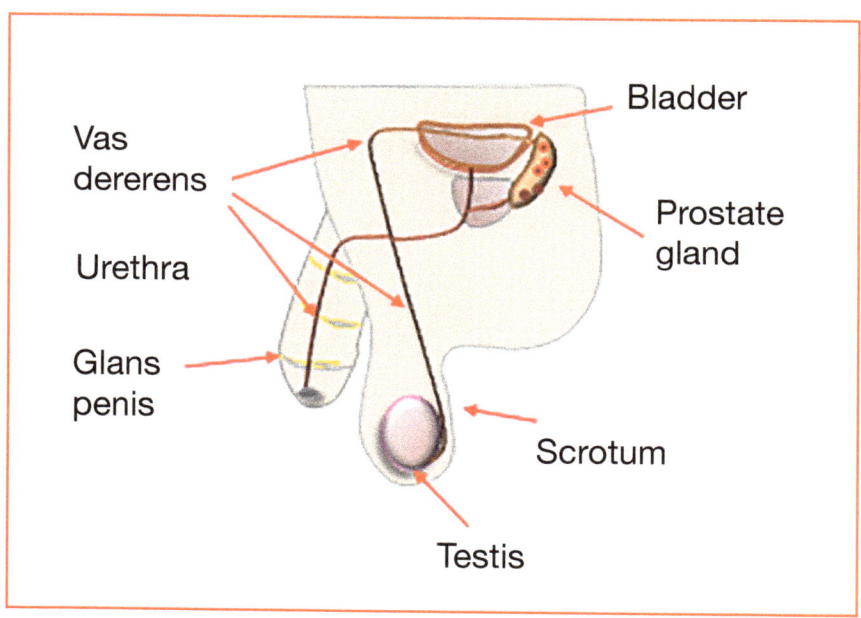

HORMONES - HOW? AND WHY?

Each of the four books identify how hormones play a major role in the changes we each experience when going into puberty and growing up. In this instance, young males between the ages of nine to eleven years; however, new research is suggesting that puberty can start in some young people at the age of seven years! This book is designed to make the journey of knowledge the young person gains, both enlightening and an enjoyable experience.

Throughout life, we each change differently. If a child is not made aware of its natural bodily and brain changes during these early years, changing from being a child to becoming a responsible adult can be a frightening or difficult experience to think about or face.

Between the ages of nine to eleven years, or younger, a male will start to experience changes in the way he thinks, sees the world, and feels. His body shape will also start to change. It is important for a child, to not only understand their body, but to understand that change is a natural process and is a part of life's progression into adulthood. These changes are all brought about by the activation of hormones within the human body and brain.

When hormones start to do their job in young males, pubic hair will appear on the body, around the genital area and under the arms. It is to be remembered, that hair grows on the body and protects the skin from chafing and becoming sore. It also allows the sweat to run from the body which in turn, allows the body to keep cool during sport and other robust activity.

Hormones are chemical messengers that allow us to grow both physically and mentally. Without hormones doing their job, we would not be able to live our daily lives as we do. Hormones have always worked in our bodies and brains; this has allowed the human species to develop into the people we are today.

As adults, we have the responsibility to support our children through the changes they experience.

ESTROGEN

Both boys and girls make the hormone estrogen in their bodies. Through my own research and teaching, now going into about forty years, and teaching all age groups from children at primary school to university students, and observing my own children and family members, one thing has struck me; the number of headaches children have at the onset of puberty.

I have identified this fact through my own experiences of growing up at the age of eight.

Research is now showing that low estrogen levels can contribute to light to severe headaches over this time of a child's development. There does need to be more research into this area, but we need to take more notice of a child if they say, *'I have a headache.'* If the headache persists, it makes sense to seek professional medical advice, but if a child says, please take notice.

A BOY'S PROGRESSION STAGES

Each child is born with their bodily parts in miniature. A boy is born with a penis and testicles a fraction of the size they will become once reaching maturity. Equally, this is so with our girl babies; these babies are at the beginning of stage one.

Like many suggested stages in the reality of life, there are differences. Each child is an individual person, will think, act, and learn differently. There is no 'one size' fits all model for all children. Having said that, all children worldwide, will experience going into puberty at similar ages.

- **Stage One** – from zero to six or seven years: loving: mummy and daddy (or the central carer) is the centre of their universe.

- **Stage Two** – from six or seven to about thirteen or fourteen years: dad starts to play his male role in preparing the boy for adulthood. This can be seen when the child works in the tool shed or like activities. Grandparents, trusted aunties, uncles, and friends also play a pivotal role.

- **Stage Three** – from thirteen or fourteen to being a young adult in their mid-twenties. A young person will continue to test their environment, try new ideas and new experiences. This can be a stressful time for parents and loved ones.

From the age of about eight years, the young male's testes will start to produce sperm; sperm is the smallest cell produced in the human body. The production of sperm is triggered by the production of the testosterone hormone.

Each child's production levels may vary. In early production and throughout puberty, some males will have 'wet-dreams' or release sperm while they sleep; not all males will have wet-dreams.

Releasing sperm during sleep is a natural process. This process allows the penis to be kept clean and healthy, it also allows old sperm to be removed from the testicles. Some sperm, if not released from the body, will dissolve, and go back into the body, this is a healthy process, and the body is doing exactly what it has been designed to do.

If a child experiences the release of sperm during sleep, do not criticise or ridicule, please remember, this is a natural bodily function and process, and like all natural processes, should be respected.

If your child has such an experience, talk about it. Encourage him to change his bed linen and to put on clean pyjamas or underpants the following evening. Talk quietly with encouragement. Please also remember, by doing small jobs like keeping his bed clean will also help in his brain development and will serve him well in his adult years.

This is a stage where the genitals will start to change and become larger. The penis and testicles will start to grow into their adult size. With the release of testosterone, and as previously said, *'hair may also start to appear around the genital area and other parts of the body.'*

HOW KIDS LEARN – DEVELOPING LIFE SKILLS

As parents, carers, and educators, the boundaries we put into place for our children in the 21st Century should include the understanding of:

- ✓ **Free Will**
- ✓ **Reasoning**
- ✓ **Consciousness**
- ✓ **Respect**
- ✓ **Awareness**
- ✓ **Empathy**
- ✓ **Responsibility and**
- ✓ **Diligence**

From each of the above familiarities, please, consider the learning all children need to start gathering from the age of twelve months. Gathering such information should be within a child's everyday living environment, if it is not, it is not difficult to start to introduce each of the above ways of thinking. This can be done at story time or in everyday interaction with the child as it learns and grows.

A child's brain is always ready to undertake new learning, so let's take each of the above one at a time.

Free Will means that children are born with the freedom of choice. Children need to understand the difference between taking or making a good to a wrong choice; this is Free Will and is an essential life skill for adulthood.

Within **Reasoning** is the choice of Free Will. Children need to understand that within the choices they make, they are using their power of Reasoning.

Within Free Will and Reasoning there is a consciousness taking place in the thinking the child does. As the child grows up, though they might understand Free Will, there is a responsibility that exists to using Free Will.

When a child is young from the ages of six months to a year, there will only be fragments of these important life skills gathering and taking place.

Consciousness is an early learned skill by all children. Consciousness is part of a child's survival instinct and of stimulus and response. To give you some idea of this, a child knows when it is hungry and needs to be fed.

Respect is learnt and has guidelines within its meaning. Children will use their Free Will, Reasoning and Consciousness when understanding that Respect has guidelines, boundaries, and a sense of power within its meaning. Respect is a learned behaviour and carries with it the limitations that allow all people to live within their family, community and or chosen country.

Awareness is the behaviour that allows a child to evaluate, give consideration, and the knowledge that understands Free

Will, Reasoning, Consciousness and Respect are to be woven into the thinking they do, their words said, or actions taken.

Empathy is the understanding that all people have feelings and each person's feelings should be respected.

Responsibility is the installing of the value that every action taken, or word spoken has an outcome and that each belongs to the child.

Diligence is a time of contemplation, commitment to the good of each: Free Will, Reasoning, Consciousness, Respect, Awareness, Empathy and Responsibility.

Life skills also include the adaption and willingness to learn new ideas, working hard and honestly to make situations work for both themselves, their families, and the wellbeing of their communities.

ESTABLISHING HEALTHY HABITS

Through learning, we have the ability, to teach our young people the qualities of life. This does not mean we teach them one way of thinking; it means we give them the mental tools to make their own right decisions. We do not take their learning from them, it means, we contribute to giving them quality learning through:

- Establishing respect for all people while working with workable guidelines.

- Establishing and taking the responsibility for the actions or words they say. If for instance you say, 'No' it should be taken for what it means, 'NO'. 'NO' is not a bad word; it is short, succinct and means what is said.

- Establishing regular meal and going to bed at a regular time each night only with minor exceptions to late nights.

- Establishing that screens and devices are only used after three years of age and for short thirty-minute daily intervals or less.

- Establishing from the age of five, the use and limited screen-time of one hour or less each day.

During a child's early development, it needs to flex its eyes to long and short distances, this builds eye muscle strength. Allowing a child to use a screen too soon, will contribute to weakening eye muscles and possibly future eye problems.

A child's pre-frontal cortex of the brain does not start to develop until six months after birth and takes a further five or six years to develop and eventually matures in their mid-twenties. Interference with the developing brain brought on through too much screen time, stress, cruel experiences or treatment, abuse, arguments, or threatening situations can interfere with young pre-frontal brain development.

- Establishing that a child needs to have creative and inventive play from its early development and before it starts to crawl.

- Establishing eating whole, good food habits from the time the child eats solid food. Whole good food does not have destructive, dead food additives added. Some food additives found in children's food may be derived from petroleum, coal tar, plastic, and other non-digestible substances; this can have a detrimental effect on the young and growing brain and result in other ill health problems, learning difficulties and behavioural problems, either now or in the future.

Remembering that whole food drives positive healthy growth and productive learning.

- Establishing gross motor skills like using a broom, wiping dishes and other household chores.

Science is showing that children, boys, possibly more so than girls, when shown how to do simple household chores early on in their life, from about the age of four or five years, or earlier, they develop self-sustainability skills in caring for themselves later in life. Simple skill development in this way helps in brain development. Scientists aren't sure of why this happens; this research is ongoing.

A motto to learn to live with: 'Don't take the learning from the child.'

YOUR BOY AND HIS BRAIN

Though the previously mentioned stages may be met at the suggested chronological age, the young boy's brain may take longer to grow into maturity.

As a young male matures into his teenage years, through his own internal drivers, he will be forced to explore his environment. He is learning to become a man. At this stage he wants to build competence, survival skills and is learning to become a fair and balanced young adult.

When a young person reaches the age of about twenty-five, the brain is now working with all its architectural structures in place, and with the neuron pathways and connections firing as they should.

Neuron brain connections of both girls and boys continue to grow and mature; some will die and be replaced by new pathways, neurons, and their connections; this is especially so, when a child goes on to do extra learning either through learning a trade, academic studies, and other learning within sport, art, and other endeavours.

Change and growth are a natural process of the human body, brain, and mind. The human mind is always hungry for new information.

ACTIVE HORMONES, PERSONAL HYGIENE, WELLBEING, AND PUBERTY

Active Hormones

Hormones are activated through the central nervous system and sends out a message to the hypothalamus, 'CHANGE'. This release is Gonadotropin (GnRH) from the hypothalamus which is sent to activate the necessary hormones at the body's right time. When gonadotropin reaches the pituitary gland at the base of the brain, that produces two other hormones, follicle-stimulating hormone (FSH) and luteinizing hormone (LH). Once reaching puberty, these hormones are released in larger quantities.

Personal Hygiene

Sweat and oil producing glands may become active at the same time as puberty onset. This may produce clogged glands, resulting in pimple, acne, or skin breakouts. By washing your face twice, a day; showering every day, especially after strenuous exercise or sport, wearing clean under clothes and keeping your body clean, it will help to reduce pimples, and body odour. Pimples can appear on the face, back, front of the body, arms, and legs. If a problem occurs and there are concerns, always speak to a dermatologist or health professional.

Wellbeing

Most adults[3] walking on the planet earth have not missed out in going through puberty.

Both boys and girls go through this stage of life, it is a natural life progression and is about reproduction and the continuation of humankind. It is to everybody's benefit that our young adults learn as much as possible about this stage.

When hormones start on the journey to activate different parts of the body, adolescent males will start to feel a sense of wellbeing and aliveness, this should not be diminished but celebrated.

Hormonal changes in both boys and girls can lead to emotional changes in behaviour. What was once a well-behaved child may appear to become a stroppy child that answers back, gives cheek and can, at times, be rude. There is no excuse for this behaviour and do not let the time slip, remind the child of who they are and what you expect of them, and one thing is not rudeness. Do not let a bad behaviour habit establish itself, if it is allowed, the behaviour patterns could follow into adulthood and cause more problem behaviour later in life.

---

[3] Absent puberty is a condition that requires professional medical advice from qualified health professionals.

Puberty

Puberty is about growing and 'Change'. It is about young people gaining their independence but gaining it so that it enhances their lives and does not lead to irresponsible actions or words.

Puberty is also about hair growth on the body, including arms, under arms, genital area, legs, and face. As puberty establishes itself, hair may become thicker, denser, or curly.

A sign of puberty may be the legs, feet, and arms become gangly in young males, but this is a natural process with the head and torso catching up as male maturity settles in. During this time, boys will add to their muscle density and mass, whereas girls may intensify in body fat.

In young males, puberty also includes the voice changing or cracking and has a deeper tone; this too, can happen at different stages in puberty.

Some young males may develop tender breasts or a slightly elevated breast shape. As the body grows and establishes itself, any breast elevation should decrease; if there are concerns, always seek professional medical advice.

ROLE MODELS AND MENTORS

The role of quality role models and mentors in your child's life cannot the emphasised enough.

During all stages of a child's development, both boys and girls, it is important to include within both their family and friend contacts positive role models.

As previously said, only include those people you can trust with your child which may include, grandparents, aunties, uncles, older cousins, or trusted friends. Such people will give your child a positive person to speak to when they have concerns; this may not be you. Do not be alarmed if it is not you. When a child seeks other trusted adults to speak to, it is a healthy sign that the child is growing and will want eventually to be in control of their own life.

Different people come from a different perspective in life and will possibly take each situation differently, and without emotion and may work to a different level. Such role models allow your child to build positive self-esteem, build independent points of view and are always a 'safe place' in times of stress or conflict.

UNDERSTANDING HOW THE HUMAN BODY GROWS AND MATURES & RELATIONSHIPS

'Changes' Meeting the National Curriculums of Australia and the United Kingdom

HORMONES WITH HATS
CURRICULUM OBJECTIVES – AUSTRALIA

Incorporating and supporting Year 4 to 6, ages 9-11 years. Personal, Social and Community Health (ACPPS070 – ACPS076 - ACPPS071 - ACPPS072 - ACPPS073 – and other related areas of the Curriculum including: COS3.3, DMS3.2, INS3.3, TLF-IDM021182 Scootle.edu.au).

MEETING CURRICULUM OBJECTIVES – UNITED KINGDOM (UK)

Natural body changes for boys between School Years 4 to 6, ages 9 to 11 years.

(Health and Wellbeing, Relationships, and Living in the Wider World)

Relationships Education, Relationships and Sex Education (RSE) and Health Education.

'Effective RSE does not encourage early sexual experimentation. It should teach young people to understand human sexuality and to respect themselves and others. It enables young people to mature, build their confidence and self-esteem and understand the reasons for delaying sexual activity. Effective RSE also supports people, throughout life, to develop safe, fulfilling, and healthy sexual relationships, at the appropriate time.' [4]

---

[4] Relationships and Sex Education (RSE) (Secondary) - GOV.UK (www.gov.uk) Extracted from 'statutory guidance Relationships Education, Relationships and Sex Education (RSE) and Health Education & Australia: https://www.scootle.edu.au

ONLINE SCHOOL PACKAGES

Full Potential Training offers a range of education packages, with our school packages for 'CHANGES', Children Growing Up, we cover the sensitive area of puberty and the changes that naturally occur in males and females. The story book at the beginning of each book allows the child to become familiar with the role that hormones play in making these body changes happen.

For young males with the ages of nine to eleven years, we have developed, 'CHANGES' Facing Kian. The girls' book is 'Changes' Facing Rosie. The books have been developed with discretion and to allow the child to quietly absorb the story board about the changes they are either going through or about to go through. We cover many sensitive areas of the subject of puberty, and how the female and male body works as the change occurs.

We offer a complete online package, which includes the story book. The online education packages do include the changes that both males and females go through during the time of puberty. They are not directed to one sex but both males and females. Once ordered, the package is downloaded from our server to the school, college, or holiday programme at your location.

The Package for Changes, Females and Males, Children between the ages of 9-11, children have one by two hours sessions, and children between the ages. 11-14 has four by one-hour sessions, including a continuous 'voice over' with each slide. There are pause times for discussion and some question-and-answer sequences.

We ask that courses be ordered at least two (2) months in advance, this allows us to print and deliver the children's books to your location and in time for the lessons.

Please keep in mind, all children are different and learn differently, the information on how the human body changes as children grow and mature, may vary from home to home and each person's perception of growing up can be different. Our books and courses are well researched with only up-to-date information included in the contents of the books and education programmes.

The package meets both the Australian and United Kingdom objectives within Social Community Health and Relationship and Sex Education.

For more information, please email,

admin@fullpotentialtraining.com.au
Or, see our website, www.fullpotentialtraining.com.au

FAMILY PACKAGES

For many people, discussing puberty and the 'Changes' that take place within the human body are private discussions. They may not be easy discussions to have, but it is a necessary part of a parent's responsibility to their child or children.

For those people, we have developed Family Packages that include one book and a CD that is the same as the School Package.

If this allows you to discuss this topic with your family in private, please contact, admin@fullpotentialtraining.com.au

Or, see our website, www.fullpotentialtraining.com.au

Thank you for reading 'Changes' facing Kian,

For the follow-up book,

Please see Changes Facing Jai

11-14-year-old boys

Published by How2Books

www.ingramcontent.com/pod-product-compliance
Lightning Source LLC
Chambersburg PA
CBHW062042290426
44109CB00026B/2702